Living With Dietary Fructose Intolerance

Living With Dietary Fructose Intolerance

A Guide to Managing your Life With this New Diagnosis

Judy Smith, a Fellow DFI Patient

ISBN : 1-4196-3149-7

To order additional copies, please contact us.
BookSurge, LLC
www.booksurge.com
1-866-308-6235
orders@booksurge.com

Living With Dietary Fructose Intolerance

Table of Contents

Prologue

I am a fellow Dietary Fructose Intolerance patient and a reading specialist, so when I was first diagnosed in the fall of 2003, I immediately began to look for information on this new condition, but found very little. Having learned to manage the hard way, through trial and error, I decided to use what I have learned to help others with this challenging diagnosis. I sincerely hope that this guide will help you understand your condition and live as "normal" a life as you can. Keep in mind that your diagnosis could have been much worse.

Yes, I know what it's like to suffer pain, gas, or diarrhea after eating. The extent of these symptoms made me wonder if I would be able to continue teaching, as running to the bathroom in the middle of a lesson is out of the question. Imagine the impression I would make on my students if I simply ate the wrong thing for lunch. The pain and humiliation were overwhelming at times. I was always a healthy person, priding myself on eating whole foods, fresh fruits and vegetables, and buying organic whenever possible. However, in my early 40's I began having unexplained symptoms. It gradually became worse and seemed to be connected to food, but I couldn't find a pattern as the same symptoms didn't happen after every meal. I had numerous inconclusive tests before the fructose breath test showed that I was fructose intolerant. As it turns out, more than half of people who were previously diagnosed with Irritable Bowel Syndrome have proven positive on the Fructose Intolerance Test, according to research done by the University of Kansas Medical Center and the University of Iowa Hospitals & Clinics.

While it was certainly a relief to finally know what was causing these symptoms, I needed to know what to do about it, and that information was very difficult to find. My doctor gave me some initial information and a diet to follow, but I was reacting to some of the things that I thought I could eat. After two years of personal research and experimentation on the topic, I want to share with others what I have learned in an effort to make your life more pleasant. I hope what you read in the following pages will help you get through this adjustment. It is also my hope that people will become more comfortable talking about this condition with others, possibly spreading the word, so that those who are struggling in silence will get this simple test done. As difficult as this is to live with, it is better than not knowing what the problem is.

As you read, please keep in mind that these are not "clinical trials" but my own experiences. I am an educator, not a doctor, which is why I am trying to help you learn how to manage. You will need to pay close attention to your own body to find out the level of tolerance that you have to those foods we are told not to eat. For now, just know that you are not alone in your suffering and try to take charge of your life by learning as much as you can about what you can and cannot eat comfortably.

What is Dietary Fructose Intolerance?

Dietary Fructose Intolerance is a relatively new diagnosis. Thanks to research done at the University of Kansas Medical Center and University of Iowa Hospitals & Clinics, we now know that many people who had previously been diagnosed with Irritable Bowel Syndrome are actually Dietary Fructose Intolerant (DFI), which is different from Hereditary Fructose Intolerance. This means that we have difficulty digesting fructose. Instead of digesting it, we produce hydrogen and methane gas, which causes pain, gas, bloating, gurgling, or diarrhea.

Fructose is a simple sugar found naturally in fruits and many vegetables. It is also the main ingredient in high fructose corn syrup (hfcs), which is used in many commercially prepared products, including juice, soda, condiments, bread, soups, sauces, etc. Most of us who are Dietary Fructose Intolerant (DFI) cannot tolerate other forms of sugar either, which makes life very challenging. Carbohydrates are a problem, as they are also sugar, but a more complex sugar, adding to our list of intolerant foods.

Gastroenterologists are being encouraged to give patients with these symptoms the fructose intolerance test. This test is quite simple and painless. It involves drinking a sweet liquid and breathing into a breath analyzer. For the fructose test, a reading of more than 20 parts hydrogen per million indicates an abnormal level of hydrogen being expelled. Some people are more sensitive than others, but it doesn't usually take long to get the correct diagnosis and it is worth knowing what is wrong.

Treatment at this point involves eating those foods that you can tolerate. Simply stated, it is a low-carbohydrate, low sugar diet. The low carbohydrate piece is due to the digestion process that turns carbohydrates into sugar, much like a diabetic diet, but with different results/symptoms. The low sugar is especially important regarding high fructose corn syrup, but also includes other sugars such as brown sugar, molasses, confectioners sugar, etc. We cannot tolerate many sweeteners. Unfortunately, many of us also cannot tolerate sugar substitutes, which may cause diarrhea. For me, sugar substitutes have always caused heart palpitations, so I avoid them for that reason as well.

This is a learning experience, and often not a pleasant one. Intestinal problems are not a popular topic of discussion and we often feel isolated. This can be such a serious problem that many people have had to change their work situations and lifestyles because they are not able to function in a particular setting. With the proper diet, as hard as it is, you should be able to continue a "normal" lifestyle. In addition, some people find that digestive enzymes help, too. That is something to discuss with your doctor and experiment with on your own.

Many of us wonder what has caused this to happen in our lives? Some people think that we are just not built to handle all of the sweeteners that our modern diet includes. Others say that some of us lose our enzymes as we age; yet there are many young adults with this intolerance. I hope that researchers can find the answer and perhaps develop some easier treatments in the near future. But for now, let's be thankful that we know what the problem is and learn to live with it. Again, it could be worse.

Getting Your Diet Under Control

To eat or not to eat...

That is the question. I became afraid of food, something I had always enjoyed. There didn't seem to be a pattern to the pain. I couldn't connect bacon with tomatoes or bread, yet each of these seemed to make me react. How could those foods possibly make give me pain? The worst humiliation was the instant and uncontrollable diarrhea. It was as if little men in my intestines pulled a cord and just sent everything flying, sirens wailed but I couldn't hear them. Now I understand that my body sees these foods as "poisons" and is doing its best to rid them as quickly as possible. After enough "events", I knew I couldn't live like this, so I returned to the doctor for more tests. Little did I know that the welcomed diagnosis would present another set of challenges. Unlike Lactose Intolerance, there was no little pill they could give me and I needed more information.

Read your food labels! High Fructose Corn Syrup is the biggest problem for us and it is in more foods than you can imagine. Things that seem healthy or harmless, like fruit yogurt, breads, even condiments like ketchup, all have hfcs. Read the ingredients and the sugar content. You'll be amazed at what you learn. For example, commercially prepared salad dressings, such as ranch, will have a wide variety of ingredients. Even foods that claim no sugar added often have untolerated sugar alcohols in them like Maltitol or Erythrytol, or versions of these, which may not agree with you. Spend a few extra minutes comparing labels in the store to find the ones that do not have hfcs or high sugar content. Check out the list of sugars included in this guide as sugar comes in many different forms. I know you're thinking you need to be a chemist to understand these labels, and you are probably right, but this should get you started.

Even when cooking for ourselves, we face challenges. Many of us cannot tolerate flour, especially when used as a thickening agent in sauces or gravies. I find that a small amount, usually 1-2 Tablespoons doesn't bother me, but any more than that, such as in a roux will give me an immediate reaction. You may want to experiment with using other thickening agents such as soy protein or rice flour to see if you can tolerate those. There are some "not starch" thickeners on the market that you may want to try, too. Otherwise, stick to roasted, grilled or stir fry meals (without sauces) to avoid problems. There are a variety of recipes later in this guide that may help you in getting started.

Bread is another problem for us. There are many hidden sugars in commercially processed breads. In your bakery section you may be able to find some that are better for you, but it is still a good idea to limit the servings per day. I've included a bread recipe in this guide if you want to try making your own. At least then you know what is in it. Toasted bread is often more easily tolerated. You can find some brands of English Muffins in your grocery store, usually in the refrigerated section, that have less untolerated sugars in them. Again, read your labels. I also keep my list of untolerated sugars in my wallet as they all start to sound the same and I am not a chemist and have learned the hard way that some of these sugar alcohols can be just as toxic to me as molasses.

The Diet

EAT:

Dairy products: Milk, cheese, eggs, plain yogurt, and sour cream.

Meat : Beef, chicken, pork, lamb and seafood (as long as it is not marinated or processed, like cold cuts).

Vegetables: asparagus, celery, chives, dandelion greens, endive, escarole, green or wax beans, lettuce, mushrooms, spinach, swiss chard, and turnip greens. Broccoli, brussel sprouts, cabbage, cauliflower, cucumbers, green peppers, radishes, summer squash and zucchini may be ok depending on your tolerance.

Starches: Potatoes, pasta, noodles, white rice.

Breads: usually white, homemade or bakery, without high fructose corn syrup or high sugar content (in minimal portions). Some people find they do better with toasted bread.

English muffins (without hfcs)

Crackers: soda crackers or saltines without hfcs.

Cereal: Cooked or low sugar ready to eat (like Cheerios)

Condiments: Butter, margarine, oil, mayonnaise (without hfcs/sugar), dressings without sugar/hfcs or high amounts of vinegar.

Desserts: low sugar cheesecake, butter cookies (containing tolerated sugar), cream puffs (see recipe section), selected ice cream (such as Breyer's Lactose Free Vanilla which contains granulated sugar and dextrose), small amounts of dark chocolate, dietetic desserts (if you can tolerate them-some sugar subs cause diarrhea).

Beverages: milk, water, tea, coffee, club soda, or diet soda.

Spices: salt, pepper, basil, oregano, paprika, thyme, rosemary, mustard, sage, savory.

Note: limit carbohydrate intake, especially breads, to 1-2 servings per day.

DO NOT EAT:

Breads: any containing hfcs or other untolerated sugars, especially dark breads that usually contain molasses or brown sugar.

Meats: Bacon or cold cuts cured with sugar (or containing sodium erythorbate, which is made from sugar).

Vegetables: beets, carrots, corn, eggplant, garlic, onions, peas, sweet potatoes, tomatoes, turnips, winter squash. You will have to experiment to see what bothers you.

Fruits (some people can tolerate small amounts of berries).

Desserts: Those containing untolerated sweeteners.

Beverages: Soda or fruit juices

Condiments: Anything with vinegar, soy sauce, or lemon juice (small amounts may be ok such as that found in some mayonnaise or mustard).

Spices such as chervil, coriander, dill weed, garlic, ginger, hot chili pepper, onion, parsley or pumpkin pie seasoning. Choose brands that do not have sugar fillers.

The University of Iowa Hospitals & Clinics has a wonderful website about DFI. They have more foods listed that you may be able to tolerate. However, I have found that I react to some of the things on their list so I am limiting this to that which I know works for me. I have also found that I may not have a reaction to a food every time I eat it, or the reaction may be minor one time and major the next. I encourage you to check out their list and see what works for you.

Again, you need to experiment with what you can or cannot

tolerate. I highly recommend keeping a chart for a month and listing everything you eat and your reaction. My reactions usually occur quickly, within 20-30 minutes, and may only be loud gurgling. However, it alerts me to the possibility that worse might happen, so I avoid eating risky foods in public places. Certain foods seem to cause more of an "explosion" than others, but there also seems to be a build up at times, so I encourage you to be very careful and keep copious notes. You may not have as fast a metabolism as I have, so monitor closely.

Other Sugars

As you read labels, you will see some unfamiliar words, unless you are a chemist. It can be confusing as we should avoid Maltitol, but Maltose is tolerated. Many of these are sugars. Sometimes it is just easier to avoid any processed foods and make your own. However, many people do not enjoy cooking, so here is a list that may help you in deciphering those food labels.

Sugars that may be tolerated (monitor your reaction carefully):
Barley malt syrup
Brown rice syrup
Dextrin
Dextrose/glucose
Glycogen
Isomaltose
Lactose
Maltodextrin
Maltose
Moducal
Polycose
Sucrose (cane sugar)

Sugars to avoid:
Agave syrup
Brown sugar
Caramel
Fructose
High fructose corn syrup
Honey
Invert sugar
Karo light corn syrup
Levulose
Maple Syrup
Molasses
Palm sugar
Sodium erythorbate

Sugar Alcohols to Avoid:
Erythrytol
Hydrogenated starch hydrosalate
Isomalt
Lactatol
Lactitol
Maltitol
Mannitol
Sorbitol
Xylitol

Sugar Substitutes: Avoid Splenda, but see how you do with others.

Seeing a Nutritionist

I highly recommend meeting with a nutritionist who has experience working with people who have Dietary Fructose Intolerance. That is how I found out about vinegar. I couldn't understand why I would have terrible pain and gas after a spinach salad with vinaigrette dressing. My nutritionist also told me that I may find it difficult to digest whole grains rather than white, so I try to get the bakery white breads without sugar or hfcs. The University of Iowa list says that we should be able to eat vinegars other than apple cider vinegar, but I have had trouble with others, too, so I avoid it as much as possible. I do seem to be ok with the amount in mustard or mayo.

Potatoes: my new best friend!

Meanwhile, I was losing weight like crazy and truly frightened about my overall health. I was looking anorexic and felt weak. I was 5'9" and 125 pounds. The Nutritionist suggested that I eat more potatoes so the starch could hold things together long enough to get more nutrients from my food. God bless her! I began to stop losing weight. I had been afraid to eat many potatoes because they are a carbohydrate, and carbohydrates are sugar. However, potatoes are a complex carbohydrate, which is a long chain of simple sugars linked together and we seem to be more able to digest these. Imagine my delight when I could have baked, fried, mashed or home fries! Apparently, old potatoes are better than new potatoes, so I avoid new red potatoes. You should limit the amount of potato the same as you do bread products since they are both carbohydrates.

This starch, or complex carbohydrate, idea also pertains

to pasta and rice. I do find that I do better with pasta than rice, maybe because rice is more of a whole grain, but you need to monitor your system. The problem is that you need to find non-tomato sauces for the pasta (see recipe section) and most canned sauces have hfcs. It is worth making your own Alfredo sauce as the canned versions also have garlic, onion and various ingredients that you may not be able to tolerate.

As with everything else, you must experiment and see what works for you. I can't stress that enough. I am extremely sensitive. I hope you are not. I encourage you to see your family doctor yearly and have annual blood work done in addition to taking multivitamins and supplements. We have to work a little harder to maintain good nutrition levels.

DFI Friendly Brands/Products

Pepperidge Farm: English Muffins, some breads
Martin's Potato Rolls
Duke Mayonnaise
General Mills Cheerios
Carr's Table Wafer Crackers
Kraft Carbohydrate Well Ranch Dressing (check all dressing labels carefully)
Breyer's Vanilla Lactose Free Ice Cream (contains sugar)
Lipton's Alfredo Pasta Sides
Walker's Pure Butter Shortbread Rounds (contains sugar)

It is important for you to take control and read labels carefully, testing various products on yourself. You are better off buying a product that has a small amount of table sugar in it as opposed to other untolerated sugars. Check the sugar content to be sure it is a minimal amount. There are many more brands that you may find agree with you, but it will vary from region to region throughout the country. These are just a few to get you started, but again, I encourage you to avoid processed foods as much as possible and to read all labels carefully.

Meal Suggestions

For those of you who do not enjoy cooking, you may find that it is now worth the effort. Cooking lets you have control of what is going into your body. Processed foods are not something we can easily digest because of all the added ingredients, so we really need to avoid using them. Overall, you may even be eating healthier in one way by not having so many processed, chemical foods. Think of it as a new challenge. If you are not the main cook of your household, try to bring that person on board. Maybe this could be something you do together. Try to make the best of a bad situation.

Breakfast:

Hot cereal: oatmeal, cream of wheat, grits (all without sugar).
Cold cereals that are low in sugar (Cheerios, Rice/Wheat Puffs, Shredded Wheat).
Crustless Quiche: spinach, mushroom, veggie (see recipe section)
Omelets: plain, cheese, mushroom, veggie (depending on your own tolerances)
Sausage Strata (see recipe section for homemade sausage)
Home Fries (no onion)
Eggs, any style, with homemade sausage patties

Lunch:

Green Salad with grilled chicken (with tolerated dressing)
Tuna or Egg Salad on greens or low carbohydrate/no hfcs bread.

Baked Potato with cheddar cheese and sour cream (no bacon bits)

Macaroni and cheese (homemade)

Dinner leftovers if you can microwave at work

Homemade soup with crackers

Snacks:

Potato chips (regular, not baked, and unflavored)

Crackers (Carr's Table Water Crackers or others without sugar/hfcs) and Cheese (hard cheeses or cream cheese without seasoning)

Peanuts* (plain or salted-read labels as some have sugar added)

Appetizers (see recipe section)

*The University of Iowa food list says peanuts other than pistachios are to be avoided, but I eat them frequently without any problem. Monitor your own reaction carefully.

Dinner:

Meats or seafood (plain, some mild seasonings may be ok but no commercial marinades)

Potato: baked, fried, mashed or as a salad

Pasta (make your own white sauce rather than tomato sauce)

Macaroni and Cheese

Rice

Veggies: asparagus, green or wax beans, celery, spinach, collard greens, and lettuce.

Some people do fine with broccoli, cabbage, green peppers, cauliflower or squash/zucchini, but you need to experiment yourself as these may cause gas.

Dessert:

Sugar free Jell-O or pudding (if you can tolerate sugar substitutes)

Sugar free ice cream or cookies (again, only if you can eat sugar substitutes)

New York style cheesecake (see recipe section)

Breyer's Lactose Free Vanilla Ice Cream (contains sugar, not hfcs)

Pure Butter Shortbread Cookies (great with a cup of tea)

Cream puffs (see recipes)

Enzymes and Supplements

Unlike lactose intolerance, there is no little pill that we can take right before eating to make us able to digest fructose...yet. I certainly hope someone out there is working on it. For now, however, I have found that taking Acidophilus and Enzymes for Digestion (found at your local vitamin and nutrition stores) seem to help. I don't have as much pain and can sometimes tolerate a food item with regular sugar in it, as long as it doesn't have much. It is also important to take a fructose free/sorbitol free daily multi-vitamin as we often are not getting the right amount of nutrients from our food. You may wish to consult with your Gastroenterologist if you are unsure about which vitamins would help you. As always, be sure to read the label on vitamins/supplements to be sure there are no fructose items in it such as derived from papaya or other fruits. Taking these supplements 30 minutes prior to each meal will give the best results. Good luck!

If you are experiencing frequent symptoms, especially diarrhea, you may have a loss of electrolytes, particularly potassium and sodium. Nutritional deficiencies may cause you to feel fatigue or weak. It is important to have your blood checked to monitor your mineral levels. Meanwhile, you might see if the following home remedies (from the University of Iowa website) help:

Recipe #1: 2 c. water
¼ t. Morton's light salt
¼ t. baking soda
3 T. dextrose
1 pkg. Unsweetened Kool-Aid

Recipe #2 2 c. diet Sprite
       ½ t. baking soda
       2 c. water
       4 T. dextrose
       ½ t. Morton's Salt

Note: Try substituting club soda for the diet drink if you do not tolerate sugar substitutes.

Cheating

Yes, this is a very difficult diet to follow. The reality is that you will want to eat things that you shouldn't. Don't ever do this when you are not at home. The results could be disastrous. When you need to feel "normal", here are a few ideas that may help you.

Fruits: Try small amounts of raspberries or strawberries, grapes, or various melons after you have strictly followed the diet for 4-6 weeks. If you have no reaction, you may be one of the lucky ones who can tolerate some fruits.

Chocolate: Dark chocolate (60% cocoa or higher), in very small amounts, might be ok for you. I'm talking about one small serving now and then. If I do this regularly I will have a problem. Read ingredients as they vary.

Homemade desserts: Experiment with homemade puddings or cheesecakes, cutting back on the sugar, or substituting with dextrose or stevia, if you like. These not only have low sugar, but low amounts of flour, too.

Whipped cream (homemade) with very little or no sugar is a nice topping for sugar free desserts.

Vegetables: Broccoli, cabbage, cauliflower, and brussel sprouts are all gassy veggies, but you might be ok with them. Try one at a time. Cooked is always better for us than raw as the cooking process causes a loss of free sugars.

Big NO-NO's: High Fructose Corn Syrup, onions, garlic, vinegar, sauces (especially with a roux), and things cooked in lemon juice or any of the above ingredients.

These are my "explosion foods". I know these are the really hard ones to avoid. I love onions and garlic! Most foods have some of these items in them, but they really bother many of us, as they also affect the other foods that are cooked in/with them. Ok, I know what you're thinking. I can't live without garlic and onions is the first response people have when I tell them what I can't have. But, come on, you can do this! Be positive! Who needs garlic anyway? There are lots of other spices, some of which you can even eat! Get creative and experiment with different spices to create new recipes. Then share them with the rest of us, ok? University of Iowa has a great newsletter that they put out with recipes that people like us send in. This is going to become a very common problem. Maybe you will come up with a great new dessert for all of us!

Dining Out

Dining in Restaurants:

Dietary Fructose Intolerance can really take the fun out of food! However, as with all things that are out of our control, we must try to make the best of it and look at this as a challenge. Remember that this is a condition that you can live with. It could be worse. Lots of people who see how thin I am, wish they had what I have. I know it's easy when you don't have to live with it. There's a big difference between "can't eat" and "won't eat". So, sometimes I just remind myself how lucky I am not to have to worry about those extra pounds and tell myself that the money I'm saving on dessert, or that restaurant meal, can go towards a new outfit!

All kidding aside, dining out is one of the most difficult times for us. It is torture to look over a menu and try to find something that isn't marinated or sauced, etc. I often just want to cry as my mouth waters for all of those things that I wouldn't dare eat in a public setting. However, we just have to pull it together and try to come up with something we can tolerate, for the sake of the people you are with. No reason to ruin their dining experience or make them feel guilty as they eat that Bloomin' Onion or that chocolate volcano sundae. Go home and have a piece of cheesecake (recipe section-it freezes really well).

This has been quite a learning experience. I have had times when I ordered mashed potatoes and a grilled chicken or shrimp, only to find out that the potatoes have garlic, or lemon butter is all over it. Not all ingredients are listed on the menu, so it is important to ask. I have found that it is easier to bring my own hamburger bun (stop laughing!) than to take a chance on the one the restaurant uses. Some rolls/breads have more hfcs than others. I have had reactions immediately after eating burgers so now I ask to see the bag that the rolls/buns come in so that I can be sure. Let me tell you, a burger without a bun is not a burger. The safest thing to do is order plain chicken or steak and ask that it be grilled on foil as the grill often has the remains of marinated meats on it and you may be unable to tolerate it. Also, many restaurants rub their meats with a blend of seasonings that may not agree with you, so you need to ask about that. Baked potatoes are usually safe but ask about french fries. Some places use spices in their fries that you may not be ok with. Even vegetables are sometimes cooked in untolerated foods, so be sure to ask. You also want to avoid breaded meats/seafood as the breading often has hfcs or the flour may bother you.

Test your tolerance to condiments like ketchup and mustard at home. Be aware that different brands have different ingredients. Find the ones that best suit you. Most have hfcs or vinegar and you may not be able to tolerate that either. If you are ordering a salad, get the dressing on the side so that you can limit the amount you use. Most restaurants are happy to help and will check labels on dressings, etc., for you, but you may wish to bring your own dressing.

Whenever possible, I prefer to have friends come to our house for dinner rather than meeting at a restaurant. I guess you could call that an "avoidance technique", but it works for me. Dining out can be one of the most depressing experiences we have. Just think of the money you save by eating at home. You can entertain at home, spend less, and still enjoy your friends.

Dining at Friends' Homes:

This can be just as difficult as eating out because you feel like a pain in the neck asking for special treatment, but if you don't, you may insult the hostess when you don't eat anything she has prepared. Worse than that, if you eat something you shouldn't and have a reaction.

Upon accepting invitations from casual acquaintances/business associates, you can try one of two things. You can eat before you go and pick at whatever is there that you can eat. If there are a lot of people, you can get by without eating much and nobody will notice. For smaller gatherings and sit down dinners, it is best to explain at the time of invitation and ask if you can bring something. The hostess may then be able to adjust the menu in some way that will work for you. Just having a baked potato available would help. If they are having marinated chicken breasts or steaks, ask that they keep one out of the marinade or offer to bring your own. Try to insist on bringing something that goes with the meal, such as pasta or potato salad, green salad, etc. so that you will know what the ingredients are in that dish. If the main course is a casserole, ask what is in it. Again, offer to bring something that will complement that dish. It can be awkward but it is worth knowing and not having a reaction in public. I find that people are very understanding and willing to make small accommodations.

Dessert is usually off limits. You may find that this is an area where you can contribute as well. Try some of the desserts I've included in the recipe section. Your close friends will not be insulted by your lack of sampling the various foods, but you also don't want them to feel sorry for you, so you must slap a smile on your face and learn to channel the conversation away from you and food and on to more interesting topics.

Alcoholic beverages present another challenge. While we may be able to tolerate small amounts of alcohol, the mixers are another story. Some suggestions include mixing with diet/club soda or water if you prefer hard liquor drinks. If you prefer wine, it must be a dry wine, nothing sweet. Experiment at home to avoid problems and BYOB if you feel more comfortable when going to someone's home. Beer and fruity tropical drinks are typically not an option, sorry guys! The best bet is to stick with diet drinks, unsweetened tea, water or club soda. You can always be the Designated Driver!

Websites & Resources

There are numerous matches for Hereditary Fructose Intolerance when you do a search, but Dietary Fructose Intolerance is a whole different problem. These sites, especially the first one, may be helpful to you in understanding what you have and how to deal with it. Hopefully, as word gets out, there will be more information available.

www.uihc.uiowa.edu/FRUCTOSE/DietBasics.htm This is the University of Iowa's Health Center where much research has been done on Dietary Fructose Intolerance. The site contains detailed lists of recommended foods and those that should be avoided. While this is very helpful, you still need to monitor your own tolerances. Be sure to read the Fructose Newsletter section, as there are many good suggestions, including recipes and brand names that may not have hfcs.

www.medhelp.org/forums/gastro/messages/36313a.html has a Q&A forum for gastroenterology patients.

Http://my.webmd.com Go to their Diet & Nutrition Department for articles on Fructose Intolerance.

www.newswise.com/articles/2002/FRUCTOSE.ACG. html Contains an article from Oct. 2002 from the American College of Gastroenterology that may be of help to you.

Recipes

The following recipes have been adjusted to meet my dietary needs. My family has tested them all over the last few years and given their approval. This is a basic "getting you started" guide. Keep in mind that you may need to make adjustments to these recipes based on your own tolerance levels. I use fresh ingredients whenever possible, although I use dried herbs unless stated otherwise, but you can use fresh by simply tripling the amount called for in the recipe.

I have found that some low fat products have ingredients that I cannot tolerate. However, if you are on a low cholesterol diet, you will need to adjust accordingly, substituting low fat/part skim products for cheeses, or using low fat half and half rather than heavy cream, margarine instead of butter, olive oil whenever possible. Use good judgment, read the labels, or consult with your physician. As I mentioned earlier, it is a good idea to have your blood tested annually for cholesterol levels. However, many people find that their cholesterol improves when following a low carbohydrate, low sugar diet.

It is important to vary what you eat. I find that although I can tolerate some broccoli, if I eat it several days in a row, I react. If you sauté mushrooms too long, they may bother you, so just cook them until lightly browned, and use olive oil rather than butter. If you like to take leftovers for lunch, try freezing them in individual containers to avoid having the same thing day after day. You can vary your meals so that you are not eating cheesy or creamy foods every night. Try grilling or doing stir-fry in between and having steamed or roasted veggies with cheesy meals.

I have found that I can tolerate small amounts of granulated sugar in some food items. However, I cannot tolerate foods that are processed in sugar, especially brown sugar, molasses, maple, and certainly not hfcs. You need to read labels carefully for ingredients and sugar content. Watch for ingredients that are made from sugar, such as sodium erythorbate. When buying bakery breads, they may contain a small amount of sugar, which should be ok, but read the ingredients carefully. Dextrose seems to be tolerated well by many of us. You may be able to find sugar free hot dogs, bacon or sausage but be careful that they do not have other types of sugar or sugar substitutes, which you may not be able to tolerate. I prefer to make my own sausage but you may be able to special order from some meat markets. Know your body and learn to listen to it.

If a recipe calls for Cream of Celery or Cream of Mushroom Soup, try planning ahead so that you have your own homemade version available. The canned versions have a lot of non-tolerated ingredients and may bother you. If the recipe calls for condensed cream soup, the results of using your own homemade will change the texture somewhat. I often buy chicken when it's on sale and make my own chicken broth to keep in the freezer, which allows me to make cream soups or use the broth in recipes. You can freeze the broth in containers of varying sizes and just pop them in the microwave to thaw quickly. It really isn't that time consuming and well worth the effort.

You may find that you cannot tolerate any kind of gravy or sauce. However, if you can handle some, you should avoid cornstarch when making soups or sauces that require thickening. Use white flour rather than cornstarch, or add potatoes (see recipes). Avoid recipes that have more than 2 Tablespoons of flour as a thickener. Try substituting soy protein or rice flour wherever possible (up to 1/3 of the amount of flour called for). There is also a thickener made from kudzu that is available in many natural food stores that you might want to try. These thickeners may change the consistency and flavor, so you will need to experiment with it.

Breads present another challenge. I find that I need to

minimize my intake of bread products to 1-2 servings per day. You might want to use the cream puffs as a bread and fill with tuna or egg salad for lunch. Use saltine crackers or wafer crackers for tuna or egg salad instead of bread at lunch, or to give more substance with soups. Make your own breadcrumbs from the ends of bread you can tolerate and keep in a plastic container in the freezer. Most packaged breadcrumbs have hfcs.

Sugar substitutes are a problem for many of us, so another product that you may want to try is Stevia. It is a plant product that is somewhat sweet. You can find cookbooks for using this product at natural food stores. Stevia comes in different forms/ strengths so you will need to educate yourself on its use.

I encourage you to get creative with these recipes. Try to put the fun back in your food by using herbs or various cheese products, if you can. Substitute other vegetables that you like and can tolerate. I know that all of these recipes would taste better with garlic or onions, but that is a big problem for most of us. As you get to know what your body accepts, look through your old favorite recipes and adjust them to suit your needs. My family is very Americana, as are these recipes, so adjust them to your liking. You may even find that your taste buds now appreciate more herbs and spices than you realized.

In addition to these recipes, we enjoy basic grilled or oven baked meats, steamed or roasted vegetables, and baked or mashed potatoes. You can get creative with herbs and spices, used minimally and rubbed on steak, pork tenderloin or chicken, then baked or grilled. Avoid purchased sauces that contain high fructose corn syrup, and other untolerated sugars and spices.

Breakfast Foods

Crustless Quiche

1 10 oz. frozen chopped spinach, thawed and drained (squeeze out liquid)
4 oz. sliced mushrooms
2 cups shredded Swiss cheese
2 cups heavy cream or half and half
5 eggs
salt and pepper to taste

Preheat oven to 350. Spray a 9" glass pie plate with cooking oil.

Toss together spinach, mushrooms, and cheese in pie plate, evenly distributing ingredients. Beat eggs and cream together with whisk and pour into pie plate. Sprinkle with salt and pepper. Bake for 35-45 minutes or until lightly browned and knife inserted in center comes out clean. Let cool a few minutes before serving.

Optional ingredients: Use other types of vegetables that you can tolerate, such as leftover asparagus or broccoli. You may want to add cooked sausage (without untolerated sugars), crabmeat or shrimp.

Sausage & Cheese Frittata

8 oz. bulk sausage (homemade)
5 eggs
¼ c. milk
¼ c. grated cheddar cheese
¼ t. salt
dash pepper

Preheat oven to 350 degrees. In an 8 inch cast iron skillet, brown sausage, crumbling with spatula as it cooks. Remove from heat. If there is a lot of grease, drain off excess, leaving enough to help eggs not stick to pan. Whisk together eggs, milk and spices. Pour egg mixture over sausage. Sprinkle with cheese. Bake in oven for 15-20 minutes until set.

For variety: cook chopped green pepper with the sausage.

Omelets

3 eggs
1 T. milk
1 T. butter
¼ c. chopped green peppers
½ c. chopped mushrooms
¼ c. shredded cheddar cheese

Whisk together eggs and milk and set aside. Preheat nonstick 8" skillet over medium-high heat. Melt butter in pan, rolling pan around to spread butter. Sauté peppers and mushrooms until slightly tender, stirring often. Pour egg mixture over veggies, being careful to keep veggies evenly distributed. Cook until slightly firm and edges begin to curl up. Gently lift the edges and let some of the egg mixture run under the omelet and cook a bit longer. When omelet is firm enough to handle, flip it over and sprinkle cheese on top. Continue cooking until bottom seems cooked. Fold in half, remove from heat and serve. You may wish to sprinkle additional cheese on top.

You can use other vegetables, sugar free bacon or ham, or just cheese, if you prefer. Some people like to add spices that they can tolerate, such as basil.

Sausage Strata

Prepare the night before serving:

2 pounds bulk sausage (see homemade recipe)
½ cup chopped green pepper
2 t. prepared mustard
12 slices tolerated bread, crusts removed
1 lb. shredded Swiss cheese
6 eggs
4 cups milk
1 t. Worcestershire sauce
salt, pepper and nutmeg to taste

Grease a 9 x 13" pan. Sauté sausage and pepper. Drain. Stir in mustard. Layer bread, sausage mixture, and cheese. Repeat. Beat eggs, milk, Worcestershire and spices. Pour over strata. Cover and refrigerate over night. Bake uncovered at 350 for 40-50 minutes.

Buttermilk Bread

2 pkgs. dry yeast
1 T. sugar
½ cup warm water
4 cup bread flour
1 T. salt
3 T. melted butter or margarine
1 ½ c. buttermilk

Combine yeast, sugar and water in a small bowl and allow to proof. In a large bowl, mix salt, butter and buttermilk. Add yeast mixture. Gradually add flour, beating after each addition. Knead until dough is smooth and elastic, adding small amounts of flour if needed. Put in greased bowl, cover with a towel, and let rise about one hour. Punch dough down, knead slightly, and form into a loaf. Place into a buttered bread pan, cover with a towel, and let rise again (about one hour). Preheat oven to 375. Bake for 35-40 minutes or until hollow sound when tapped. Brush top with butter while still hot. Cool before slicing.

Soups

Chicken Broth

1 broiler/fryer chicken (about 3 lbs.)
2 stalks celery
salt and pepper to taste

Clean chicken and place in large pot or Dutch oven. Cover with water. Cut celery into large pieces (maybe 2 or 3 sections per stalk) and place in pot. Sprinkle salt and pepper. Cover and bring to a boil over medium heat. Turn down to simmer and cook until chicken is tender (about 1 hour). Remove chicken to cool and debone (freeze chicken meat for future meals). Strain broth. Use immediately or freeze for future use.

Tortellini Soup

5 c. chicken broth
1 c. chopped celery
1 10 oz. pkg. frozen chopped spinach
2 c. frozen cheese tortellini
1 egg
3 T. grated Parmesan cheese
¼ t. salt & ¼ t. pepper

Thaw or cook spinach in microwave. Drain and squeeze out excess moisture. Set aside. Heat broth and celery to boiling. Add tortellini and cook until tender. Add spinach and heat through. Mix egg, cheese, salt and pepper together. Slowly stir into soup. Sprinkle each serving with additional cheese.

Note: When shopping for tortellini, read ingredients carefully as they vary greatly.

Option: Add 1 c. of cooked chicken for a more complete meal. This is a good substitute for traditional chicken soup. Also, to serve more than 4, simply add more chicken broth and tortellini as needed.

Cream of Celery Soup

5 cups homemade chicken broth
1 bunch celery, chopped
2 potatoes, diced
1 c. half and half
1 c. milk
2 T. butter/margarine
2 T. flour
1 t. salt
½ t. pepper
1 T. chives (optional)

Cook chopped celery and potatoes in broth until tender, about 30 minutes. Puree in blender in small batches and return to pan. In separate pan, melt butter. Stir in flour, making a paste. Gradually add celery mixture to pan, stirring constantly over medium heat to thicken. Slowly add half and half, and then add the milk, stirring over low heat until heated through. Sprinkle with salt and pepper to taste. Garnish with chives if tolerated.

Cream of Mushroom: Sauté 16 oz. chopped mushrooms in 2 T. butter until lightly browned. Add chicken broth and simmer 5 minutes. Puree in blender as with celery soup and continue with above directions.

Hearty Potato-Broccoli-Cheese Soup

6 medium potatoes, peeled and diced
3 crowns broccoli, chopped & cooked
4 stalks celery, chopped
4 c. chicken broth
3 c. cheddar cheese, grated
1 t. tarragon
salt & pepper to taste
½ c. sour cream

Put chopped celery, diced potatoes, chicken broth, tarragon, salt and pepper, in soup pot and simmer for 30 minutes or until potatoes are tender. Mix in broccoli. Put about 4 cups of soup at a time into a blender and liquify until all soup has been processed, returning to another soup pot as you blend. Stir in cheese. Serve in bowls with a dollop of sour cream.

Note: Leave out the broccoli if you cannot tolerate it, cutting back the chicken broth to 3 cups. This will then be a hearty potato soup. You may wish to add cooked shrimp or flaked crab and mix the sour cream in directly.

Appetizers

Spiced Chicken Wings

3 pounds chicken wings
½ c. butter or margarine, melted
1 c. grated Parmesan cheese
1 T. basil
1 T. oregano
2 t. paprika
1 t. salt
½ t. pepper

Preheat oven to 350 degrees. Line a shallow baking pan with heavy-duty foil and spray with cooking oil. You can cut the wings into drumettes, for easier eating, or leave them whole. In a shallow bowl, combine Parmesan cheese with spices. Dip each wing in butter, then in seasoning mix. Arrange on pan. Bake for 1 hour.

Note: The inexpensive pre-grated cheese works best.

Crab-Stuffed Mushrooms

1 lb. fresh mushrooms
1 (6 oz.) can flaked crabmeat
2 oz. cream cheese, softened
¼ c. mayonnaise
¼ c. grated parmesan cheese
3 T. fresh thyme
¼ t. ground pepper

Preheat oven to 325 degrees. Wipe mushrooms clean and remove stems. In a bowl, combine remaining ingredients. Spoon crab mixture into mushroom caps and arrange in a large roasting pan. Bake 45-50 minutes.

Note: Use the mushroom stems in omelets or quiche the next day.

Sausage-Stuffed Mushrooms

2 lbs. mushrooms
1 lb. sausage, bulk and sugar free
½ c. breadcrumbs
1 t. oregano, dried
1 t. basil, dried
salt & pepper to taste

Wipe mushrooms with dry paper towel and snap off stems. Melt 2 T. butter or margarine in large skillet and sauté caps for a few minutes, turning so that both sides are lightly browned. You can be doing this while cleaning the mushrooms so that you are doing one skillet full at a time. Place gently cooked caps in a baking sheet with sides, bottom side up, and set aside.

Sauté sausage until browned and place in bowl. Chop mushroom stems and saute them until tender. Put stems in bowl with sausage. Sprinkle breadcrumbs and spices on top and mix together. Fill caps with sausage mixture.
Bake at 350 for 15-20 minutes or until lightly browned.

Option: Sprinkle grated parmesan cheese over mushrooms while still hot.

Spinach Triangles

1 Pkg. Frozen Stouffer's Spinach Soufflé, thawed
   1/2 Pkg. Filo dough, thawed (I use Athen's brand-other
brands may give more strips per sheet)
   1 stick Butter, melted (do not substitute margarine)

Work quickly with Filo dough, or keep a damp cloth over
unused portion to keep it moist. Lay wax paper on counter or
cutting board. Lay one layer of Filo dough on paper and brush
with melted butter. Repeat with two more layers. Using a pizza
cutter, cut dough into five strips, the length of the shorter width.
Place a teaspoon of soufflé mix (or mushroom mix below) at
one end of each strip. Fold like a flag to make a triangle. Place
on jellyroll pan or cookie sheet with sides. Repeat this process
until dough/soufflé are used. Brush tops with additional butter.
Bake at 400 for approximately 10-12 minutes or until light
brown. Makes about 35.

Options: For large gatherings or just to add variety, saute
1 lb. Mushrooms, finely chopped, in 1 T. olive oil until tender.
Mix in ¼ c. fresh thyme, ½ t. salt, ¼ t. pepper, and 6 ounces
mascarpone cheese. Use this filling for the other ½ of the
package of Filo dough. These should be baked at 375 for 8-10
minutes or until golden.

Sausage Stuffed Filo Cups

2 boxes prepared Filo cups
1 lb. bulk sausage (see homemade recipe)
1 c. grated cheddar cheese

Brown sausage. Drain well. Mix ¾ c. cheese gently into sausage while still hot. Scoop into cups. Sprinkle with remaining cheese. Briefly place in preheated 350 degree oven to melt cheese on top.

Other options: Add 8 oz. sautéed chopped mushrooms to the sausage.

Asparagus Rolls

20 thin sliced bread, crusts removed (without hfcs or other untolerated sugars)
3 oz. blue cheese (or closest size available)
8 oz. cream cheese, softened
1 egg
20 asparagus spears (1 can or use freshly cooked)
½ lb. butter or margarine, melted

In small bowl, mix cheeses and egg. Melt butter in pan or microwavable container. Roll bread flat on cutting board. Spread cheese mixture on bread (about 1-2 T. per slice). Place asparagus spear in center and roll up like a hot dog. Cut each bread roll into three smaller rolls. Dip in melted butter and place on jellyroll pan or cookie sheet with sides. Repeat with rest of bread and asparagus. Freeze. Place in bag for future use. When ready to serve, bake at 400 degrees for 15-20 minutes or until lightly browned.

Hot Crab Dip

2 (8 oz.) cream cheese, softened
1 c. sour cream
¼ cup Mayonnaise
1 lb. fresh crabmeat (see note below)
1 c. shredded Cheddar cheese
1 t. chives
¼ t. salt
¼ t. pepper
1 t. dry mustard
1 T. Worcestershire sauce

Mix together all ingredients except crabmeat. Fold in crabmeat. Pour into 7 x 11" baking dish. Sprinkle with cheddar cheese. Bake at 350 for 35 minutes or until bubbly. Serve with crackers (without hfcs). Serves a large crowd.

Note: Crabmeat can get expensive, so I sometimes substitute a combination of canned crab combined with either real or imitation crabmeat. This recipe is very popular with my non-DFI friends.

Crabbies

1 package English Muffins (no hfcs)
8 oz. Velveeta cheese
1 stick butter/margarine
2 T. Mayonnaise
1 can crabmeat, drained

Soften butter and cheese. Mix together with mayonnaise. Add crabmeat and mix. Split muffins into halves then cut each half into quarters. Spread the cheese mixture on each muffin piece. Freeze on cookie sheet. At this point you can put into a bag for future use. When ready to bake, place pieces on top rack of broiler pan. Broil frozen pieces until brown and bubbly, watching carefully, as they burn easily. Makes 48 pieces.

Vegetables & Side Dishes

Sautéed Asparagus

1 bunch fresh asparagus
1 T. olive oil
salt & pepper to taste

Heat oil in 12" skillet. Trim asparagus, cutting off tough ends. Add asparagus to skillet. Cover and cook over medium-high heat for about 7 minutes, shaking pan to stir every few minutes. Sprinkle with salt and pepper. Serve immediately.

Options: After cooking, add 1 t. toasted sesame seeds.

Note: This can also be done with fresh green beans. Just cut off the tip and leave them long. Use about a pound of fresh beans or enough to serve 4.

Spinach Soufflé

1 10 oz. package frozen, chopped spinach, thawed
2 T. butter or margarine, melted
3 large eggs
1 c. milk
1 c. freshly grated Parmesan or Romano cheese
2 T. flour
½ t. salt
¼ t. nutmeg
¼ t. pepper

Drain spinach, squeezing out excess liquid. Mix with melted butter. In a large bowl, beat eggs with flour and spices. Whisk in milk and cheese. Stir in spinach mixture. Pour into lightly greased 8 inch square baking dish. Bake at 350 degrees for 30 –35 minutes or until set. Let stand 5 minutes before serving.

Cheesy Potato Bake

1 box frozen hash browns (Ore-Ida brand has 9 squares/box)
8 oz. shredded cheddar cheese
1 pint (16 oz.) half and half
1 stick butter or margarine
dash salt and pepper

Preheat oven to 350. Grease baking dish. Heat half & half with butter until butter melts. Lay hash browns in pan. Pour half and half mixture over it. Sprinkle with cheese, salt and pepper. Bake until bubbly and lightly browned, about 1 hour 15 minutes.

White Baked Ziti

Makes a great entrée for a meatless meal, too.

1 16 oz. package ziti
½ c. butter or margarine
2 c. heavy cream
2 c. grated parmesan cheese
1 c. sour cream
16 oz. ricotta cheese
2 eggs, lightly beaten
1 T. oregano
2 c. shredded mozzarella
salt & pepper to taste

Cook and drain pasta. Put butter and cream in a sauce pan and heat until butter melts over medium heat. Stir in 1 ½ c. parmesan cheese and keep stirring until cheese is melted. Do not bring to a boil. Let sauce cool a bit then stir in sour cream. Toss with pasta until evenly coated. Spoon half of pasta into lightly greased 9x13" baking dish. In a separate bowl, mix together ricotta cheese, eggs, ½ c. parmesan, spices, and ½ c. shredded mozzarella. Spread evenly over pasta. Top with remaining pasta mixture. Sprinkle with remaining mozzarella cheese. Bake at 350 degrees for 30 minutes or until bubbly and lightly browned. Serves 8.

Note: use low fat sour cream, part skim cheeses, and half and half instead of heavy cream, to lower fat content.

Easy Macaroni & Cheese

Unlike traditional recipes, this has no flour.

4 cups milk
1 ½ c. elbow macaroni, uncooked
1 ½ c. grated sharp cheddar cheese
3 T. butter or margarine
salt and pepper to taste

Preheat oven to 350 degrees. Melt 3 T. butter in a 2 quart casserole dish in oven. Stir in raw macaroni. Sprinkle with cheese, salt, and pepper. Gently pour milk over everything. Do not stir. Bake 1 hour.

Basic Fettuccini Alfredo

8 oz. Fettuccini noodles, cooked and drained
¼ c. butter or margarine
1 ¼ c. light cream or half and half, divided
¾ c. grated Parmesan cheese
¼ t. pepper
Pinch of salt

Melt butter in large skillet. Stir in ¾ c. cream. Cook, stirring constantly, 2-3 minutes. Add Fettuccini to skillet. Stir in remaining ½ c. cream, cheese, and spices. Stir 1 minute. Serve with freshly grated Parmesan and pepper. Makes 4 servings.

Entrees

All recipes are designed to serve 4 unless stated otherwise. Adjust to your needs.

Cheesy Meatloaf

1.5-2 lbs. ground beef (or combination of beef and ground turkey)
½- ¾ c. breadcrumbs (from bread without hfcs)
¼ c. milk
1 egg
1 t. oregano
½ t. dry mustard
salt & pepper to taste
1 c. shredded mozzarella cheese

Preheat oven to 350 degrees. Mix together, by hand, all ingredients except the cheese. Add enough bread crumbs to hold mixture together. This will depend on the exact amount of meat that you are using. Place a piece of plastic wrap or coated freezer wrap (I prefer this) on a clean flat surface. Flatten meat mixture into a square to about 10" in diameter and about ½-¾ inch thick. Sprinkle the cheese evenly on meat. Roll up and place seam side down in a baking dish. It is much easier to do this without touching the meat if you are using the freezer wrap. Bake for 30-45 minutes or until cheese just starts to ooze out of ends and temperature is 160 (medium).

Roasted Fillet of Beef

1 tenderloin of beef (about 3 ½-4 pounds)
1 T. olive oil
Kosher salt and coarsely ground black pepper, to taste

Preheat oven to 425 degrees F. Brush the meat with olive oil and rub with salt and pepper. Place the meat on a rack in a shallow roasting pan and roast for 15 minutes. Reduce the temperature to 350 and roast 20 minutes more for medium-rare or 25 minutes for medium. Let the roast rest at room temperature for 15-20 minutes before slicing into ½ inch thick pieces. Serves 6-8.

Grilled Pork Tenderloin

2 pork tenderloins (will serve 4-6)
¼ c. olive oil
1 t. dried rosemary
1 t. dried thyme
½ t. ground sage
salt & pepper to taste

Put pork in marinading dish or zip loc bag. Mix oil and spices. Pour over pork. Marinade overnight. Preheat barbecue grill to high. Cook tenderloins, turning ¼ turn after each 5 minutes for a total cooking time of 20 minutes or until internal temperature is 170 degrees. Let rest 5 minutes before slicing.

Note: This is delicious served with egg noodles or cheesy potatoes and grilled veggies.

Homemade Sausage

1 lb. ground pork
1 T. dried thyme
1 T. dried sage
1 T. dried savory
1 t. salt
¼ t. pepper

Mix together all ingredients by hand (as you would a meatloaf). Form into cylinder and wrap in plastic wrap overnight. Slice and cook as patties or use in recipes calling for ground/bulk sausage.

You can experiment with other spices, or mix with ground veal, to meet your specific needs/likes. My family enjoys this combination both as a breakfast sausage and in the appetizer/dinner recipes. Depending on where you buy the pork, the fat content will vary. Makes 1 pound but doubles easily. I often make several pounds and put it in the freezer.

Stuffed Pork Loin

3-4 lb. pork loin
16 oz. ground sausage (without sugar)
8 oz. mushrooms, chopped
½ c. bread crumbs (no hfcs)
1 t. ground sage
½ t. salt
½ t. pepper

Brown sausage and mushrooms. Drain. Mix with bread crumbs and sage and set aside.

Slice pork loin lengthwise to within ½ inch of other side and open like a book. Sprinkle with salt and pepper. Press stuffing mix onto pork to within ½ inch all around. Roll up as tightly as you can. Tie with string and place seam side down in roasting pan. Sprinkle with additional salt and pepper if desired. Bake at 350 for about 60 min. or until thermometer reads 155 degrees. Remove from oven and let sit for 10 minutes. It will continue to cook. Carve into ½ inch slices.

I like to put peeled potatoes around the roast, turning them every 15 minutes to give a browned presence. They should be fork tender at the time roast is removed from the oven.

Radiatore with Sausage and Spinach

16 oz. radiatore pasta
16 oz. bulk sausage (see homemade version)
10 oz. bag spinach leaves
1 T. olive oil
4 oz. sliced mushrooms
1 c. shredded mozzarella
1 c. shredded parmesan
salt & pepper to taste

Place pasta in boiling water and cook 7-10 minutes until done. Drain and set aside. At the same time, brown the sausage in a Dutch oven until it is cooked through and well crumbled. At this point, add 1 T. olive oil and the mushrooms. Continue to cook and stir until mushrooms are browned to your liking. Add spinach but do not stir. Cover and cook 4-5 minutes until leaves are just wilted. Add hot, drained pasta to sausage mixture. Sprinkle with cheese and stir/toss until well blended. Add salt and pepper to taste. Serve with additional grated Parmesan cheese, if desired. Serves 6.

Option: Substitute chicken/turkey for the sausage, either with bite sized pieces or ground.

Chicken Tarragon Salad

2 c. cooked, diced chicken
1 c. chopped celery
1 c. mayo (no hfcs)
1 ½ T. dried tarragon
½ t. salt
¼ t. pepper

Stir together all ingredients, adjusting mayo to your liking. Serve on a bed of garden greens or as filling for sandwiches. This is a great use for leftover cooked chicken.

Chicken with Mushroom Sauce

4 boneless chicken breasts
3 T. butter or margarine
2 c. sliced fresh mushrooms
1 medium green pepper, cut in cubes
½ c. chicken broth
¼ t. salt
1 t. ground pepper, divided
½ c. sour cream
1 T. flour
1 T. dry sherry

Wash and trim chicken breasts. Spray large skillet with cooking oil and sauté chicken for about 2 minutes on each side. Remove from pan. Add butter to pan and cook mushrooms and peppers until tender, adding additional butter or oil as needed to keep mushrooms from sticking. Remove from pan. Add broth to skillet. Return chicken to pan, sprinkling with salt and half the ground pepper. Bring to a boil, then lower heat, cover and simmer for 5-7 minutes until done. Place in covered casserole dish to keep warm. Mix sour cream with flour, ½ t. pepper and sherry. Add to skillet. Heat and stir for a minute. Add mushroom mixture and heat through. Pour over chicken. Serve with cooked rice.

Herbed Chicken and Veggie Bake

This is a nice, low fat, all inclusive, easy meal that adjusts well to serve more people. It also smells great while cooking. Serve with a salad or other vegetables for your non-DFI friends.

1 whole chicken cut up (or about 3 lbs. pieces)
3 medium baking potatoes, sliced in 4-6 lengthwise wedges
1 pound whole mushrooms, wiped clean
1 green pepper, cut into wedges
¼ cup olive oil
3 t. oregano
1 t. salt
¼ t. pepper

Preheat oven to 400. Combine oil and spices. Set aside. Put prepared veggies in baking pan. Toss with half of the oil mixture. Place chicken parts on top of veggies and drizzle rest of oil mixture on top. Rub to spread oil/herb mixture evenly over chicken. Bake 1 hour, brushing chicken with pan juices after 30 minutes of baking. Chicken should have browned, somewhat crispy skin. Veggies should be tender. Serves 4-6.

Option: Add other tolerated vegetables for variety. I sometimes add baby carrots for my non-DFI friends and family.

Spiced Chicken Breasts

6 boneless chicken breast halves
2 T. mustard
2 T. sour cream
1 c. fresh bread crumbs (no hfcs)
2 t. chopped fresh thyme
salt and pepper to taste
1 t. vegetable oil

Preheat oven to 425. Spray a baking pan with cooking spray. Wash and dry chicken. In a small bowl, combine mustard and sour cream. In a shallow dish combine the bread crumbs and thyme. Season each piece with salt and pepper. Brush the tops of each piece with some of the mustard mixture. Dip each chicken piece, mustard side down, into breadcrumb mixture, pressing firmly onto chicken. Arrange the chicken pieces, coated side up, on the oiled baking sheet. Drizzle oil over chicken. Bake until breadcrumb mixture is brown and crisp and the chicken is cooked through, about 15-20 minutes.

Option: Sprinkle 1/2 c. grated Parmesan cheese before baking.

Chicken and Broccoli Alfredo

8 oz. fettuccini pasta, cooked and drained
2 c. fresh or 10 oz. frozen chopped broccoli
2 T. butter or margarine
1 lb. boneless chicken breasts (about 3)
1 ½ c. cream of celery soup
½ c. milk
¾ c. grated parmesan cheese
salt & pepper to taste

Cook fettuccini according to package directions. Cook broccoli in pasta water during the last 4-5 minutes. Drain. Meanwhile, cut chicken into cubes or bite sized pieces. Melt butter in 12" skillet and cook chicken until browned, stirring frequently. Add soup, milk, cheese, salt, pepper, pasta and broccoli. Heat through. Serve with additional Parmesan cheese.

Stir-fry Chicken and Veggies

3-4 boneless chicken breast halves
8 oz. sliced fresh mushrooms
1 green pepper, cut into 1" cubes
4 stalks celery, cut into ½" slices
4 T. olive oil
1 c. chicken broth
1 t. dried rosemary
½ t. dried thyme
2 T. flour
salt & pepper to taste

Cooked rice or angel hair pasta

Heat oil in 12" skillet. Sauté mushrooms, pepper and celery in 2 T. olive oil until translucent but still firm, about 5 minutes. Cut chicken into bite sized pieces. Place in Ziploc bag with 2 T. flour, herbs, salt and pepper. Remove vegetables from skillet and keep warm in covered casserole dish.

Add 2 T. olive oil to skillet, if needed, and heat. Add chicken and sauté, stirring constantly, until cooked through, adding more oil as needed. When chicken is cooked, slowly add chicken broth, stirring and scraping bottom of skillet to create sauce. Combine with vegetables. Serve with cooked rice or angel hair pasta.

Option: Use beef cut into strips and substitute beef broth for a beef stir-fry. Change the herbs to 1 t. basil and ½ t. oregano.

If flour bothers you, marinade chicken in olive oil and spices 1-2 hours. After removing vegetables, cook chicken and combine with veggies. Omit chicken broth. Sprinkle with parmesan or romano cheese.

Creamy Chicken and Biscuits

2 c. cooked, diced chicken
1 box frozen chopped broccoli or green beans
1 can cream of celery soup
1 c. sour cream
1 c. shredded cheddar cheese
6 frozen biscuits, thawed (no hfcs)

Preheat oven to 350 degrees. Grease the bottom and sides of an 11 x 7-inch baking dish. Combine chicken, vegetable of choice (thawed enough to break up), soup and sour cream. Pour into baking dish. Bake for 15 minutes. Remove from oven and sprinkle with ¾ cup of cheese. Arrange biscuits on top and sprinkle with remaining cheese. Bake until biscuits are golden brown and sauce is bubbly, about 20 minutes longer.

Note: Read ingredients on biscuits carefully. I use Pillsbury successfully.

Shrimp Bake

1 ½ lb. large shrimp, shelled and deveined (if desired)
1 ½ c. fresh bread crumbs (made from bread with no hfcs), divided
½ c. melted butter/margarine
½ lb. Lump crabmeat or 1 (6.5 oz) can crabmeat, drained and picked
2 T. mayonnaise
1 egg
½ t. baking powder
½ t. prepared mustard
¼ t. salt
¼ t. pepper
½ t. basil
½ t. oregano

Spray or grease 9 x 13" baking dish. Spread shrimp in bottom. Mix together mayonnaise, egg, baking powder, mustard and spices. Fold in crabmeat and ¾ c. breadcrumbs. Spread on top of shrimp. Sprinkle additional breadcrumbs on top. Drizzle with melted butter. Bake at 450 for 15 minutes until shrimp is pink and top is golden. Serve with rice or angel hair pasta and vegetable of choice.

Option: Place asparagus on top of stuffing mix, and then put breadcrumbs on top of that before baking.

Shrimp Stir-Fry

1 ½-2 lb. shrimp, peeled and deveined
1 12 oz. box bow tie pasta (or angel hair)
8 oz. mushrooms, sliced
1 bunch asparagus, cut in thirds
3-4 T. olive oil
1 t. oregano
salt and pepper to taste
fresh Parmesan cheese

Clean and peel shrimp. Drizzle with 1 T. olive oil. Sprinkle with oregano, salt and pepper. Refrigerate at least one hour, or overnight. Cook pasta according to package directions. Drain and set aside. Cover to keep warm.

In large skillet or Dutch oven, heat 2 T. Olive Oil. Add asparagus and cover. Cook for a few minutes, tossing gently periodically. Remove cover and add mushrooms, stirring frequently until lightly browned. Add small amounts of olive oil as needed. Remove veggies from pan and add shrimp to pan. Cook 2-3 minutes or until lightly pink and curled. Remove from heat and add pasta. Drizzle with 1 T. Olive Oil and stir gently. Grate fresh Parmesan cheese over individual servings. Add salt and pepper to taste.

Basic Grilled Shrimp

1 lb. large shrimp, cleaned and deveined
¼ c. olive oil
Seasonings: oregano, basil, salt & pepper

Place shrimp in zip loc bag. Mix oil and seasonings and pour over shrimp. Chill for 2 hours or overnight. When ready to cook, preheat grill and cook shrimp for about 3 minutes or until slightly curled and pink. Serves 2-4, depending on your appetites.

This is delicious served on a bed of baby greens.

Note: I like to use my George Foreman Grill for this but an outdoor barbecue or cast iron skillet works also.

Variation: Chicken breasts (boneless) can be marinated in this same spice and oil mixture. Cook for 5-7 minutes, depending on thickness.

Simple Herbed Salmon

Salmon filet (whatever size you need)
Olive oil
Dried thyme (or spice of your choice)
Salt and Pepper to taste

Spray heavy duty aluminum foil with cooking spray. Preheat
outdoor grill. Place salmon skin side down on foil. Drizzle with
a little olive oil. Sprinkle with salt, pepper and herbs of choice.
Seal foil tight. Place on hot grill. Cook for about 10-15 minutes,
depending on thickness, or until it flakes with a fork.

Note: This can be cooked the same way in the oven at
about 425 degrees.

Family Friendly Pizza

Proceed with caution only if you can tolerate some breads.

1 loaf "take and bake" french bread-found in your grocer's deli/bread area.
2 c. shredded Mozzarella Cheese
1 sm. can Hunt's tomato sauce (or use olive oil and herbs of choice for yours)

Toppings of choice: browned ground beef or sausage, sliced mushrooms, green peppers (for us) and sliced onions, garlic, pepperoni, etc. for our family members.

Bake the bread according to package directions, usually 10-12 min. and let cool. Slice lengthwise and again in half to make 4 pieces. Place on heavy duty foil on broiler pan. Spread 2-3 T. tomato sauce on each piece of bread. If you prefer, omit tomato sauce for yours and brush bread with olive oil instead. Sprinkle cheese. Add toppings as desired. This is the family friendly part as everyone gets to have what they want. Bake at 450 for 5-7 minutes and then broil for a few more minutes until lightly browned.

Note: Read bread ingredients carefully. You could substitute english muffins (with no hfcs) if you like. Serve with salad for a complete meal.

Desserts

New York Style Cheesecake

This is a hit even with my non-DFI friends and family. It is creamy and rich. Have a variety of topics for them to add as desired.

1 lb. Ricotta cheese
2 8 oz. cream cheese, softened
1-pint (16 oz.) sour cream
1 c. sugar
1 stick butter, melted
4 eggs, slightly beaten
3 T. cornstarch
3 T. flour
2 t. vanilla

Preheat oven to 300. Butter a 9" spring form pan. Mix cheeses together. Add sugar gradually and eggs. Add flour and cornstarch, then sour cream, vanilla and butter. Bake 1 hour 10 minutes, or until cake begins to brown around the edges. Cake may still be a bit wiggly. Turn off oven and leave cake in the oven as it cools, about one hour. It will firm up as it cools. Refrigerate, or freeze, after cake is completely cooled.

This can be made a few days in advance. Offer fresh raspberries, chocolate syrup, melted caramel, or canned cherry pie filling as a topping for your non-DFI friends, but do not put it on the cake. You can spread ½ c. sour cream on top if you like.

If using a 10" pan, turn oven off after 1 hour.

Options: Cut sugar back to ¾ c. and add 2 melted (1-ounce) semisweet chocolate baking squares to the batter. Blend in for full chocolate effect or swirl in with knife after putting batter into pan for a marbled effect.

Cream Puffs

1 c. water
½ c. butter
1 c. flour
4 eggs

Fillings: 4 c. sugar free pudding OR
               1 pt. Heavy cream, whipped until peaks form

Heat oven to 400. Heat water and butter to rolling boil in saucepan. Stir in flour. Stir vigorously over low heat until mixture forms a ball, about 1 minute. Remove from heat and beat in eggs, all at once. Beat until smooth. Drop by ¼ cup scoops, 3" apart, onto ungreased cookie sheet. Bake until puffy and golden, about 35-40 minutes. Cool. Cut off tops. Pull out any extra soft dough. Fill puffs with sugar free pudding or whipped cream. Put tops back on and refrigerate until ready to serve. Makes 12 large puffs. To make 24 small puffs place on cookie sheet by large teaspoonfuls. Recipe can be halved if serving a small group and you want to keep them fresh.

Use large puffs filled with tuna, chicken or egg salad for lunch. Fill small puffs with cream cheese mixed with shrimp or crabmeat for appetizers or get creative with fillings.

Note: Visit your local whole/natural food store where sugar free chocolate may be available. They may have other dessert options that appeal to you as well. Good luck!